Energy Ball Manual

Charles Mage

Published by Charles Mage, 2019.

ENERGY BALL MANUAL

First edition. January 4, 2019.

ISBN: 978-1393324546

Written by Charles Mage.

Also by Charles Mage

Watch for more at https://www.czchapbooks.com/.

Table of Contents

To all serious and passionate practitioners of the arts magickal...

Introduction

Creating an energy ball is an interesting subject in psychism, as well as in the occult arts.

It is an excellent way to learn how to effectively manipulate energy, and it can also do countless things.

Not to mention, it is fun to make!

Creating an energy ball is all about manipulating or controlling magickal energy.

You can then form it into a ball and even command it to do a task for you.

Isn't that amazing?

Learning to create an energy ball is also an excellent training to increase concentration, exercise your willpower, and be a more effective energy manipulator, among others.

Energy Ball Manual is divided into four parts:

Part I talks about the theory behind the creation of an energy ball.

Before you create an energy ball, you first need to be equipped with the right knowledge behind this magickal feat.

Part II discusses the actual steps on how you can create an energy ball.

Be sure to read the instructions carefully and study this how-to guide.

Do not worry, I have written it in a way that is simple and easy to understand.

Part III shares important tips and pieces of advice that you should observe to further increase your chances of success.

Part IV gives answers to frequently asked questions regarding the creation of an energy ball.

May this occult manual be your guiding light to success, happiness, peace, magickal, and a meaningful life.

Blessed be!

ENERGY BALL MANUAL

Part I: Theory

Understanding magical energy

Ancient occult teachings express the idea that everything in the universe is made of energy.

In fact, even modern science, specifically, quantum physics, has proven this belief.

But, what is magickal energy?

This magickal energy is not new.

Even in ancient times, people have used and referred to this mysterious power.

In India, it is known as prana; in China, it goes by the name of chi; in Japan, it is called ki; in Greece, they refer to it as pneuma — and so on.

Although it goes by many names, you should take note that they all refer to the same magickal energy.

This energy is the energy of the whole cosmos and the entire universe.

It is the energy of the sun, moon, planets, and stars.

Interestingly, it is also the same energy that you have inside you and all around you.

Indeed, this energy or prana exists everywhere and permeates everything.

Occult rituals and spells all revolve around being able to manipulate or control magickal energy and direct it to do the will of the magician/witch.

As you can see, learning to control this energy is an essential skill that you must have.

The good news is that creating an energy ball is one of the best and fun ways to learn this magickal craft.

From now on, you have to think in terms of energy, as everything in the universe is composed of magickal energy.

You are made of energy.

How to manipulate magical energy

Manipulating magickal energy is a skill that every serious practitioner of the magickal arts should learn.

Indeed, if you get good at it, then great things are in your hand.

So, how do you do it?

How do you manipulate magickal energy and make it form into a ball?

According to an ancient Hermetic teaching, the All is Mind and that the Universe is Mental.

Another teaching expresses that "As Above, so Below."

Although this has several occult significances, for now let us use it in relation to the creation of an energy ball.

The key that you have to remember is that you can manipulate magickal energy by using your mind.

Remember this magickal secret: *Energy follows thought.*

As a magical practitioner, you should know that the imagination is the best tool of a magician/witch.

If you look at the word closely, you can form this little code: i-mage.

Indeed, the imagination is an occult magickal tool and a proclamation of the magical self.

Unfortunately, many people fail to use the power of their imagination to its full potential.

When it comes to using the imagination, visualization always comes to mind.

For example, if I tell you to imagine a frog, you get to picture it in your mind.

Although this may be okay, you can still take it to the next level by using more senses.

Do not just see the frog in your mind.

Also hear it croaking, even smell it or feel it.

The more senses you use, the more you make it powerful and real.

Interestingly, even modern science has discovered that the mind cannot really tell the difference between physical reality and one that is only imagined.

This should not be a surprise since according to ancient magickal teachings, those that you imagine are also real.

It is only the modern world that taught man that their imagination differs from reality.

So, from now on, think as a real magician as you are and know the truthfulness of your imagination.

If you find it hard to do the usual visualization, you might like what many refer to as tactile visualization.

When you do tactile visualization, you do not use any visual or any other sensory imagination, except only the sense of feeling.

So, instead of imagining a bright burning ball between your hands, simply "feel" a hot sensation between your hands, without having to "see" a hot ball in your mind's eye.

There are people who prefer it this way.

However...

Since you are a serious and passionate practitioner of the Craft, and as far as this manual is concerned, you are my student, and it is strongly ordered that you must learn to use all senses at once.

So, do not be content with just the regular way to visualize things or with tactile visualization, but use all senses at once — for this is the way of the Magus.

Energy sources

Before you can create an energy ball, you need to draw energy from something.

You should understand that this energy is inside you and all around you.

The energy inside you is known as your personal energy. There is also the energy of the sun, moon, oceans, rocks, and stars, and so forth.

The energy all around you is referred to as the universal energy.

Do not be confused, these are all one and the same energy force, but they just vary in terms of quality and vibration.

With the power of your mind, you can draw energy from anything and everything.

It is not always good to use your personal energy since it can be draining.

If you spend too much personal energy, then you might end up drained and tired.

So, it is suggested that you draw energy from external sources.

Still, for starters, it is advised that you first create an energy ball using your own personal energy.

After that, you can then move to the next step and absorb energy from other sources like the sun and trees.

Once again, to use your own energy or draw energy from external sources, simply use your imagination.

You can visualize energy in any way you want.

If you are just starting out, it is often recommended that you "see" the energy as white light.

But then again, you are not limited to this.

If you want to see it as green or even blue water, you can do that as well.

The important thing is to know and intend that it is magickal energy that you are manipulating.

Hence, for example, if you want to draw energy from the Sun, simply visualize the Sun in the sky (You do not even have to see the physical Sun.), and visualize a ray of light coming down from the Sun and let it enter the top of your head, and then let this ray of light flow and form a ball between your hands.

Do not worry about this for now, as we will discuss in better detail the manner of creation later on.

For now, just focus on learning the theoretical side and gaining as much knowledge as you can.

Programming

Programming is a modern term but nonetheless an ancient practice.

Basically, it is all about telling your energy ball what to do.

For example, if you want to use it for healing, then you "program" it to heal.

There are several ways to do programming.

The most common and probably one of the best is by imagining that your energy ball is already doing that which you want it to do.

Hence, if you want to use it for healing, then simply imagine it over and over again in your mind that it is healing that which you want for it to heal.

Another example: If you want to use it to push a light object, then simply see it in your mind's eye again and again that it is pushing that object successfully and repeatedly.

The power of repetition is also used as it impresses the command that you want your energy ball to do.

Do not forget about this power of repetition as it is really helpful.

Another method of programming is simply by telling your energy ball what you want for it to do.

For example, if you have a headache and you want to use your energy ball for healing, simply tell your energy ball to heal your headache.

It is that simple.

For this purpose, you may want to use the power of repetition again.

As you can see, programming is actually very simple, yet it is very important to learn as it is the part where you give your command to your energy ball.

Sensing energy

Before we move on to the actual steps of creating an energy ball, it is a good idea to first learn how you can sense energy.

This way you can tell if you are really sensing or forming any energy between your hands.

The following exercise is a basic and popular way to sense energy:

First, rub your hands together for about 10 seconds.

Next, position them in front of you as if you were holding a ball.

Bring them as close as possible but do not let them touch.

ENERGY BALL MANUAL

Do not even allow your fingers to touch.

Now, as you breathe in slowly, bring your hands slowly apart.

As you breathe out slowly, bring your hands back as close as possible without letting them touch.

After a few seconds, you will start to feel some pressure and/or tingling sensation between your palms.

This is magickal energy that you are feeling.

If you do not feel anything, do not be discouraged.

Just practice this every day, and you will soon succeed.

Do not worry, this technique is very easy to learn, and you will most probably get it on your first try.

If you do not get it on your first several attempts, just keep on trying until you succeed.

Part II: Practice

Now that you know the important theory behind the creation of an energy ball, it is time to move on to the practical side of creation:

Planning

The first thing you want to do is to have a plan.

Why do you want to have and use an energy ball?

Do you want to use it for protection, healing, or just for fun?

It is your will that will be done.

There must be a purpose.

This is also the time when you can think about other details, such as for how long you want your energy ball to exist, its color, and others.

Once you know why you want to have an energy ball, then it is time to move on to the next step.

Draw energy

Place your hands in front of you as if you were holding a ball.

Now, it is time to draw energy.

Of course, you can also use your own personal energy, but it is not suggested for a reason that we have already discussed *(as it can be draining)*.

You can draw energy and let it go directly to the location between your hands where you intend to make your energy ball, but you can also allow it to enter your body before letting it flow out of your hands.

The choice is yours to make.

Be creative.

If you are drawing from the Earth, you can absorb energy from the soles of your feet and let it fill your body before you let it flow out of your hands into the energy ball.

Also, remember that you can absorb energy from the air.

You might want to do this with every inhalation.

You are also free to combine the energy sources if you want.

You can also draw energy from far-away planets since energy and imagination know no bounds.

Continue to draw as much energy as you like and have it accumulate into a ball between your hands.

You should be able to feel the presence of the energy ball between your hands at this point.

If you do not feel anything, then you need to add more and more energy until you are satisfied.

Naming (optional)

Everything in the universe has a name of some sort.

Even God who is nameless is referred to as God.

If anything does not have a name, then it does not exist.

This is true, especially in the physical world.

Hence, you should also give your energy ball a name.

You normally do this if you want your energy ball to exist for some period of time.

But, if you just want to create an energy ball and have it disappear immediately, then you do not have to give it a name.

So, how do you give it a name?

This is easy.

Simply tell the energy ball its name.

For example: "Your name is......"

Do not use a common name or a name that would be easy for anyone to guess.

If another magician or witch knows about its name, they can call your energy ball by its name and take control of it.

Indeed, names have power.

Programming

Now that you have an energy ball and that it already has a name, it is time to tell it what you want it to do.

We have already discussed how to do programming.

Once again, tell it what you want it to do or do the repeated imagination technique where you visualize your energy ball doing its task over and over again.

Since you are my apprentice as much as this manual is concerned, then you ought to do both techniques at the same time, for this is the way of the true Magus.

Timing (optional)

Just as there is a moment of creation, there is also the moment of death or expiration.

You should give your energy ball its lifespan.

This is where you set for how long you want it to exist.

To do this, simply tell your energy ball, "You have a lifetime of....."

It can be as short or as long as you want.

Just remember that if you give it a long lifespan, say a week, then you have to recharge it with energy from time to time.

To do this, simply call it by its name and visualize it in front of you.

You then feed it with more energy in the same way that you have created it.

If you do not give it a lifetime, then it will only last depending on how fast it uses up its energy, as well as the amount of energy that you have invested in it.

Let go

Now that your energy ball is complete, finally, you have to let go of your energy ball and let it do its task.

There are many ways to do this.

You can blow on it or simply toss it in the air.

It does not matter how you do it, the important thing is to know that you are now sending it out into the universe to accomplish its task.

Letting go means more than just the simple act of sending it out into the world.

It also means that you must not think about your energy ball — and this is where many practitioners often fail.

They keep thinking and even worrying about their energy ball that it fails to do its task.

The reason why this happens is that your energy ball can easily be recalled just by saying its name or even by simply thinking about it.

Hence, for it to fully do its mission, you have to let it go completely.

Do not hold on to it with your mind.

This also means that you must not think of the result or the outcome that you desire.

This is because thinking about your desired outcome connects you to the energy ball.

Again, let go.

A good trick to do is to do something and get busy.

This way you would not be thinking about it.

Once again, let go of your energy ball and let it do its mission, and do not hold on to it with your mind.

This is how you make a "miracle" unfold.

CHARLES MAGE

Part III: Tips and Advice

Now that you know how to make an energy ball, here are helpful tips and pieces of advice that you should know:

Practice regularly

Regular practice is important.

Just like learning any other skill, you have to engage in continuous practice if you want to be successful.

Energy balls are fun to make, so you would not have any problem with it.

It is very versatile and indeed truly helpful.

The best way of practice is to make creating an energy ball a part of your life.

Do not use force

When you draw energy, allow the energy to flow smoothly and naturally.

Do not force it.

It is also good to note that if you draw energy from those that have a soul like the Sun, be sure to thank the Sun for it.

Be kind and appreciate what is freely given to you.

Believe

It is so often that those who are starting out to learn how to create an energy ball fail to do so because of a lack of belief.

They just do not believe in themselves and in what they are doing.

Remember that energy follows thought.

If your thought fills you with disbelief, then no wonder it will be difficult for you to create a real energy ball.

The more that you practice and improve, the more that you can easily believe in the reality of an energy ball.

Meditation

This is often overlooked by those who practice the Craft, or at least they do not give it enough importance than it deserves.

If you are serious about learning the Craft, then you must practice meditation regularly.

The practice of meditation is an overall spiritual exercise.

It energizes all the chakras, develops concentration, and increases willpower, among others.

You do not need to engage in any complicated form of meditation if you do not feel comfortable.

In fact, even the basic breathing meditation can be of great help to the development of your magical faculties.

How do you do the basic breathing meditation?

Well, it is as simple as paying attention to your breath.

It is also known as *meditation on the breath*.

Here is a more detailed guide:

First, assume a meditative position.

It can be any position so long as you are comfortable, but be sure to keep your spine straight.

The reason why you want to keep your spine straight is to ensure the free flow of energy since the seven main chakras (energy centers) are located along the spine.

Now, just relax and breathe in and out gently.

Put all your focus on your breathing.

Breathe in and out.

Nothing must exist in your mind but the breath.

Although this breathing meditation may seem very simple, it may be difficult for a beginner.

You may find that your mind wanders a lot while you meditate.

So many thoughts can creep into your mind preventing it from becoming still and at peace.

Do not worry, because this is normal if you are just starting out.

In Buddhism, this is known as the *monkey mind* where the mind is like a monkey that jumps from one branch to another, so does the untrained mind jump from one thought to another.

Just keep on practicing, and you will get better and better over time.

Use elemental powers

If you want to take your energy ball to the next level, you can also make use of the elemental powers.

For example, if you want to have a hot energy ball or one that can give you courage, then you can make use of the quality of the element fire.

You can make a fire energy ball.

For this purpose, you might also want to absorb energy from the Sun.

If you want an energy ball that can help you relax, you may want to use the element water for its relaxing quality.

Now, if you want to improve the intellect or if you want to deliver a message, then an air energy ball is a good idea.

Finally, if you want an energy ball that can give you stability or anything physical or concerning the material plane, then you might want to use the element earth.

Of course, this is just to give you an idea.

There is so much to be said regarding the elemental powers.

But, if you are just starting out, just stick to creating a white ball of energy.

This is just to give you an idea of how you can further improve your practice of creating an energy ball.

Shell

There are practitioners who recommend using a shell.

This is not required but more of a personal preference.

The purpose of a shell is to prevent the energy ball from leaking its energy, as well as a form of protection for your energy ball.

The way to do this is to visualize a shield (shell) form around your energy ball.

Be convinced in your mind that this shell protects your energy ball.

It is that simple.

I personally do not find the need of using a shell, but then again this is a matter of personal preference, so feel free to apply whatever works best for you.

Relax and enjoy

The creation of an energy ball should not be seen or felt like heavy labor.

You have to do it with a good and positive spirit. Hence, just enjoy the process.

Do not worry, as creating an energy ball can be really fun.

So, do not be too hard on yourself.

If you fail or commit mistakes, just learn from the experience and move on.

Keep on practicing and just enjoy every second of it.

If you suddenly feel like you are being disappointed or start to feel a sense of negativity, then stop and just relax.

You do not need to rush the learning process.

Have fun as you learn.

After all, the magickal path has no end.

Take a break

Although you are well-advised to engage in continuous practice, it is also recommended that you take a good, nice break from time to time.

You should not force yourself too much.

When you feel tired, then take a rest and just relax.

However, take note that this should not be an excuse for being lazy.

Before you take any kind of break, be sure that you first engage in some practice, perhaps create an energy ball or two.

Since energy balls will now be a part of your life, it is only right and best that you do not put too much pressure on yourself.

Relax every now and then.

Also, by giving yourself time to rest, you will be able to manipulate energy more effectively.

Part IV: Answers to Questions

I really want you to learn to successfully make an energy ball, so let us now discuss the answers to frequently asked questions:

Am I doing it right?

Beginners often ask this question, and this is where the mistake occurs.

You would not want to ask yourself this question while you are making your energy ball.

The moment that you do, then that is the mistake that you need to correct.

When you make an energy ball, you want to put all your energy and focus on what you are doing.

That is not the time for you to ask yourself such doubtful questions.

You can, however, ask such kind of question *after* the magickal working, which can then give you a point of reflection, but not during the actual work.

How fast can you make an energy ball?

It is not the speed that matters.

An energy ball can be created in as fast as less than three seconds; however, you cannot expect such an energy ball to be of good quality.

On average, and for beginners, you might want to spend around 5-15 minutes in creating an energy ball.

Again, the time that you spend does not matter.

The important thing is to be able to create a useful and strong energy ball.

Why is the process of naming and timing considered optional?

For an energy ball that you will use only for a few minutes, then there is no need for you to name or give it any lifetime since it will soon dissipate on its own.

Normally, you only give me a name or lifespan if you intend for your energy ball to last for hours, days, or any other extended period.

In this regard, it does not just act as a simple energy ball but now takes the form of an elementary or a servitor, which is more of an advanced kind of magick.

If you are a beginner, skip the steps of timing and naming for now, and just focus on learning to manipulate energy effectively and creating a simple yet enjoyable and useful energy ball.

Can you make it physically visible?

This question is of great interest.

Indeed, those who have spent some time creating an energy ball to the point that they feel it like a solid ball in their hands also get a desire to make it physically visible.

But, is this possible?

The answer to this is a resounding *yes*.

However, this is something that takes practice.

If you have been making energy balls for some time, you will reach a point where you can seem to see waves in the space between your hands, just where the energy ball is located.

You do not need to look too hard to see this.

Another way of seeing your energy ball is by creating an energy ball in a dark room.

If you accumulate enough energy, it can emit light, even in the physical realm.

If you master this technique, it can be powerful enough to light up a whole room that even laypeople (those without magical training) will be able to see your energy ball.

If you want to reach this level, then keep on practicing, and you will soon succeed.

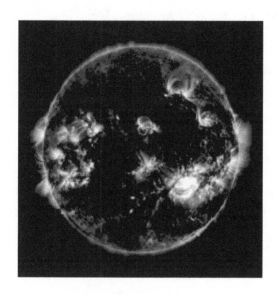

Can an energy ball move physical objects?

Yes, an energy ball can move physical objects.

You might want to try this by throwing it at an object.

You can then check how it affects the object on a physical level.

Instead of throwing, you can also use your energy ball to push an object.

It is suggested that you try to practice with a light object, such as a balloon.

If you practice enough, you can even throw your energy ball and knock down a soda can or bottle.

Remember that the only limitation is the one you impose on yourself.

If you keep on practicing and if you believe enough, then nothing is impossible.

Can I make more than one energy ball?

Yes, you are free to make as many energy balls as you want.

If you want to make lots of energy balls, it is suggested that you draw energy from an external source to avoid draining yourself of energy.

Do I have to use my hands?

No, you do not need to use your physical hands.

The instructions only tell you to use your hands only to assist your imaginative mind in the creation process, but you can create an energy ball without any physical movement and without assuming any formal physical posture.

Remember: It is your mind that creates the energy ball, for all true and genuine magick starts and ends in the mind.

Indeed, there are adept practitioners who create energy balls in public places and spellbound people with their magic.

Can I change it into a different shape?

Yes, you are not limited to shaping it into a ball.

If you want, you can turn it into a cube, triangle, or even into an airplane, and other complicated shapes.

Still, many adepts are satisfied with the ball-shaped energy construct.

This is just a matter of personal choice, with the exception that certain shapes may be used for reasons of elemental correspondences, which is quite an advanced form of magick and is not covered by this manual.

For now, just focus on creating energy balls.

I cannot sense the energy. What should I do?

Just keep on practicing.

By now, you are already equipped with the right knowledge, and it is just a matter of putting that knowledge into actual practice.

Also, be reminded that you should try to use as many senses as you can.

If you cannot feel it, then maybe you can compensate it with being able to "see" it more clearly in your mind's eye.

Again, use all or as many senses as you can, especially the sense of sight and feeling.

Keep practicing, and you will improve.

Is it just my imagination?

This is another common question.

The answer is, yes, creating an energy ball is *mostly* a mere act of the imagination, not to mention it also requires willpower and belief.

However, just because it is an act of the imagination and that it exists in your mind do not mean that it no longer exists.

In fact, for those very reasons, magically speaking, only prove that the energy ball does exist.

Remember the ancient magickal teaching that "Thoughts are things."

Last words?

Now that you know how to create an energy ball, remember to always use it for a good purpose.

The world is already torn into pieces.

Most people have already lost their humanity and have been dominated by the system of the modern world.

Be careful, and always tread on the path of love and goodness.

I hope you have enjoyed our humble magical journey.

CHARLES MAGE

With light and love, blessed be.

Did you love *Energy Ball Manual*? Then you should read *True Initiation into the Craft of Magick*[1] by Charles Mage!

True Initiation into the Craft of Magick is a complete manual that teaches the path of true initiation into the magical arts. It reveals a system of magick especially made for solitary practitioners, but even those who belong to a certain group or coven can also benefit from the teachings in this manual. Indeed, this is a manual for all witches, magicians, mages, wizards, and all practitioners of the Craft of Magick. It lays down a complete system of initiation, so that anyone who wishes to learn the real

---

1. https://books2read.com/u/mglGy6

2. https://books2read.com/u/mglGy6

and sacred practice of magick may be given a chance to discover and experience its beauty and wonder.

What does it mean to be initiated into the Craft of Magick? It means so much more than just reading about the occult arts. To be truly initiated, you should prove yourself worthy. In this manual, you will be given a special training course. By the time you finish the practices in the magical system as revealed herein, and provided you stay true to the teachings and the practices, then there will be no doubt that you would finally attain true initiation into the Craft.

It is a sad fact that there are so many people out there who claim to be magical practitioners but know so little about the Craft. Worse, their magical skills and abilities are so poor that you might think of their practice as a mere joke. This is not to offend such people, but only to point to the fact that among the many initiates out there, only a few are true and genuine.

True Initiation into the Craft of Magick teaches a legitimate magical system that can be used by beginners and even by intermediate practitioners. It is for those who are truly sincere in knowing and practicing the real Craft of Magick. This occult manual is packed with essential theories and practical exercises. Do not fear or worry, as I will guide you at every step of this journey. Just like any other art form, merely reading the techniques is not enough just as reading books about painting would not make one a painter. Take note, however, that acquiring the right knowledge is important. But, in order for this knowledge to be perfect, it has to be realized, and the only way to do this is to put your knowledge into actual and continuous practice.

This magical manual covers, among others, the following:
- The true meaning of Magick

- Important magical theories
- Magical techniques and exercises
- The magical mind and the occult power of the imagination
- How to manipulate magical energy effectively
- Meditation techniques
- The chakras
- Elemental magick
and more!

Indeed, this magical system will welcome you into the real Craft of Magick. It will transform you into a real magical practitioner, a true and genuine initiate of the Craft of the Wise. If you think that you are worthy, then be ready to learn and train magically, for it is time for you to cast the most powerful magick: cast yourself.

With light and with love, let us begin...

Read more at https://www.czchapbooks.com/.

Also by Charles Mage

Watch for more at https://www.czchapbooks.com/.